Tea, Shadows & Surprises

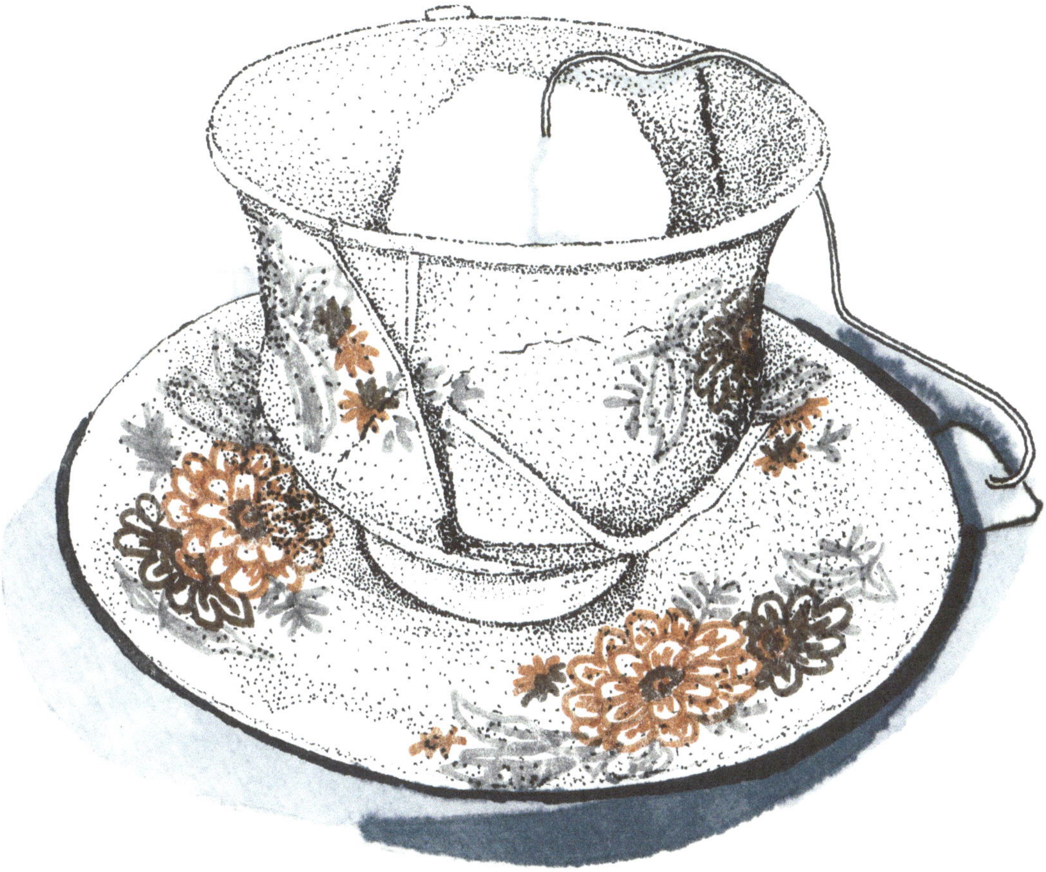

mini-comics by
Mandi Coates

Published in Canada by Engen Books, St. John's, NL.

Library and Archives Canada Cataloguing in Publication

Title: Tea, shadows & surprises / mini-comics by Mandi Coates.
Other titles: Tea, shadows and surprises
Names: Coates, Mandi, author, artist.
Identifiers: Canadiana 20210227133 | ISBN 9781774780459 (softcover)
Subjects: LCGFT: Comics (Graphic works)
Classification: LCC PN6733.C63 T43 2021 | DDC 741.5/6971—dc23

Copyright © 2021 Mandi Coates

NO PART OF THIS BOOK MAY BE REPRODUCED OR TRANSMITTED IN ANY FORM OR BY ANY MEANS, ELECTRONIC OR MECHANICAL, INCLUDING PHOTOCOPYING AND RECORDING, OR BY ANY INFORMATION STORAGE OR RETRIEVAL SYSTEM WITHOUT WRITTEN PERMISSION FROM THE AUTHOR, EXCEPT FOR BRIEF PASSAGES QUOTED IN A REVIEW.

This book is a work of fiction. Names, characters, places and incidents are products of the author's imagination or are used fictitiously. Any resemblance to actual events or locales or persons living or dead is entirely coincidental.

Distributed by:
Engen Books
www.engenbooks.com
submissions@engenbooks.com

First mass market paperback printing: July 2021

Cover Design: Ellen Curtis
Cover Image: Mandi Coates

CONTENTS

Tea for One 005
Addendum 015

Sunbeams 017
Addendum 018

Something Deep Down 024
Addendum 032

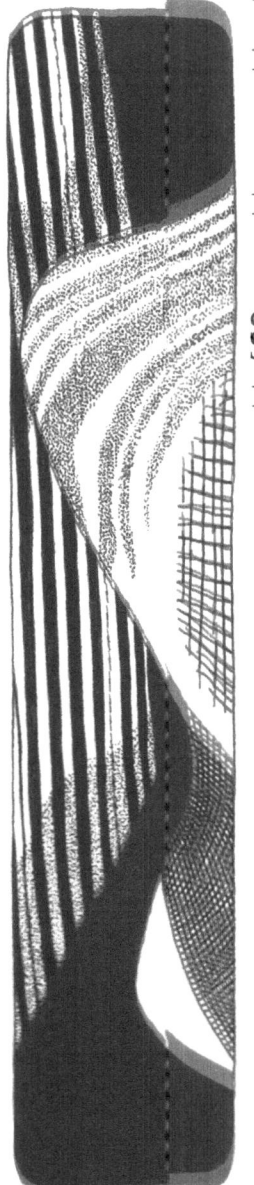
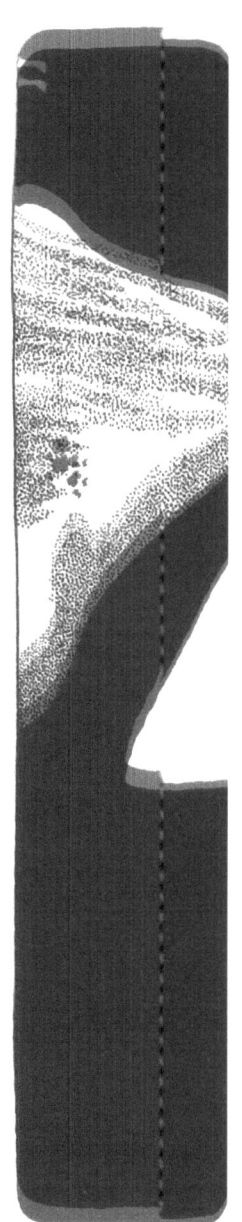

To my parents, especially my Mom, for all the love and support and instilling in me that I could accomplish anything I worked for.

To my friends Charlene Tobin, Jennifer Williams (who came up with the title), and Jo-Anne Petten (my life model for *Something Deep Down*), whose constant support and friendship have meant the world to me.

~For Nan Margaret~

60 Billion

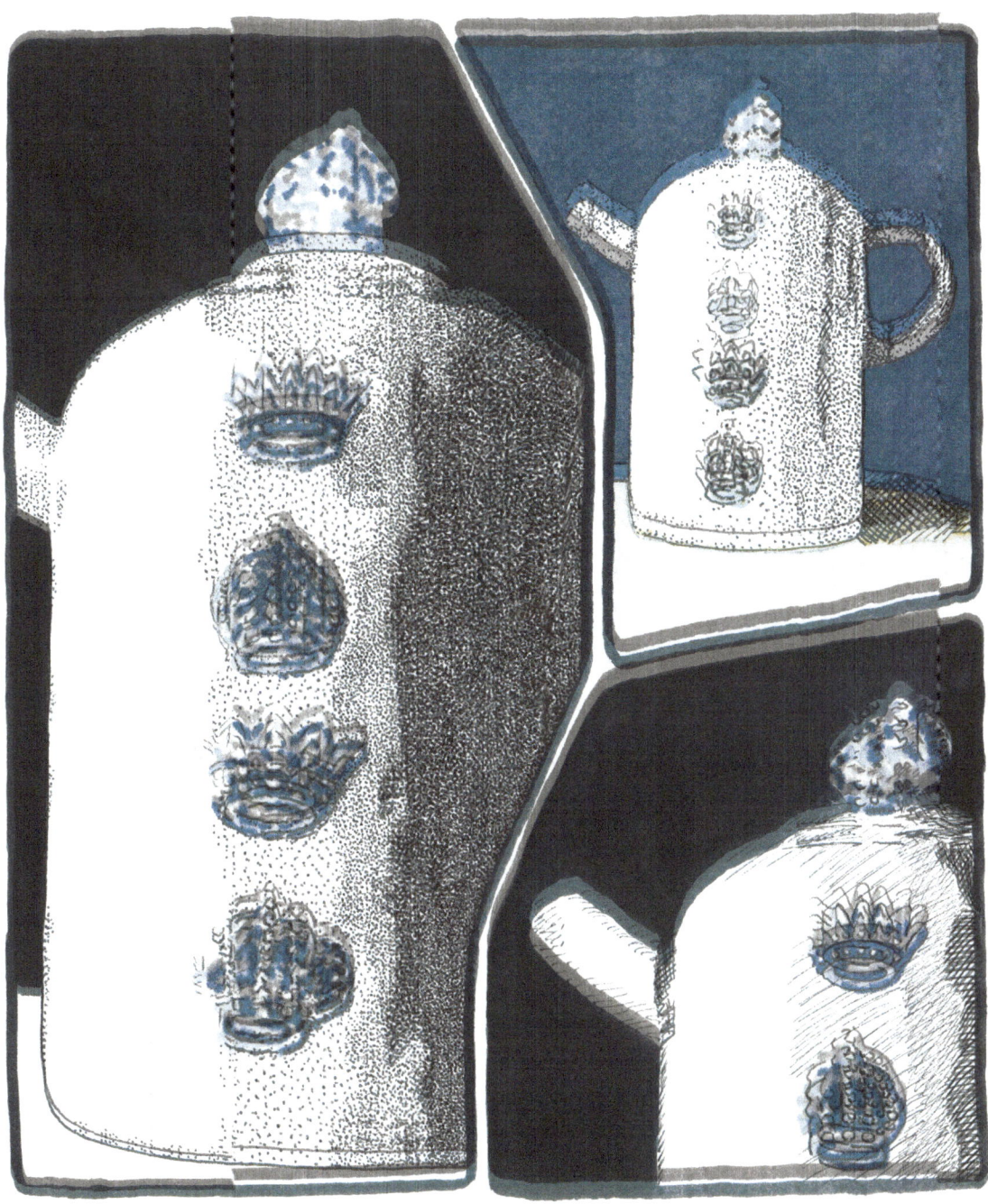

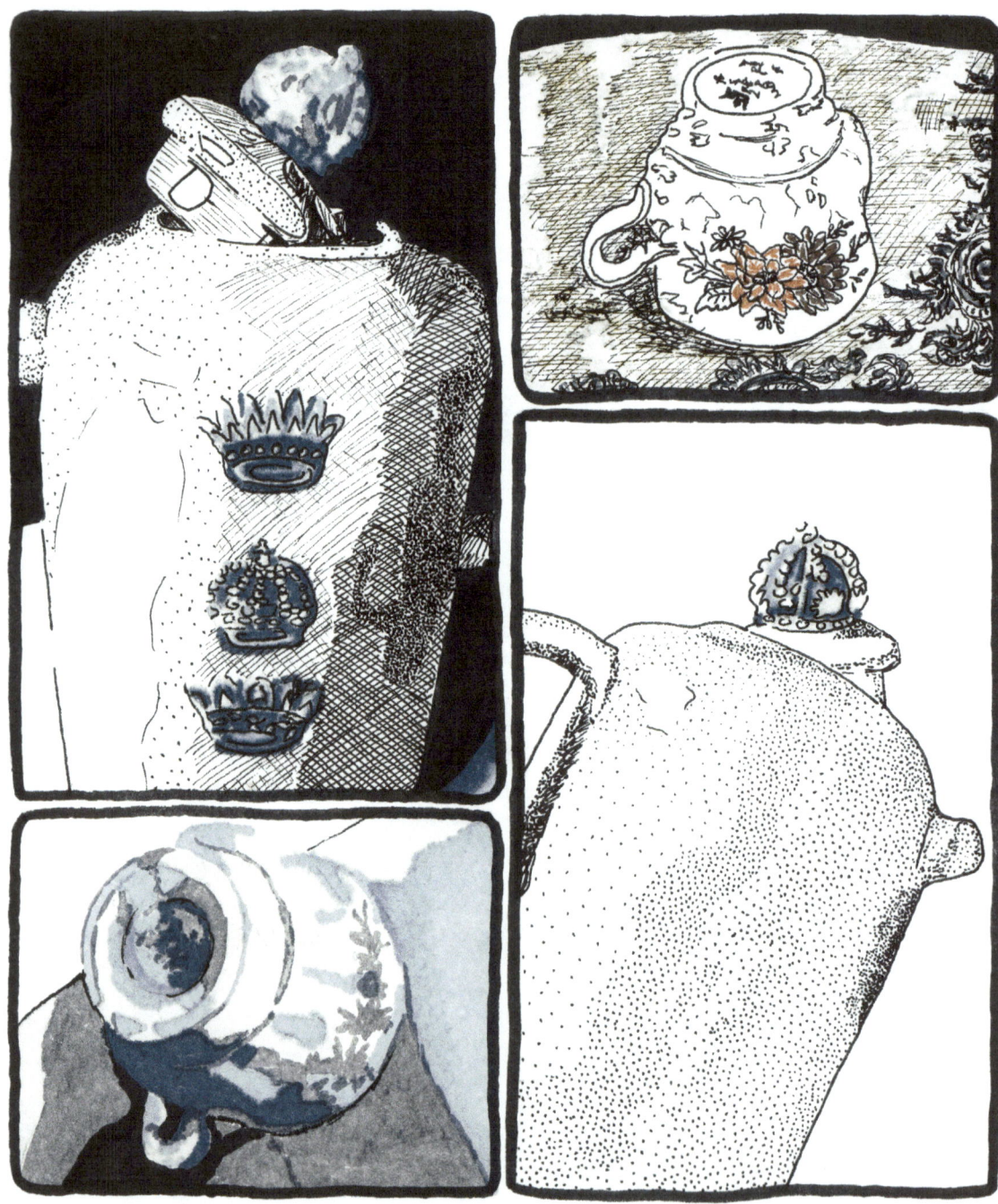

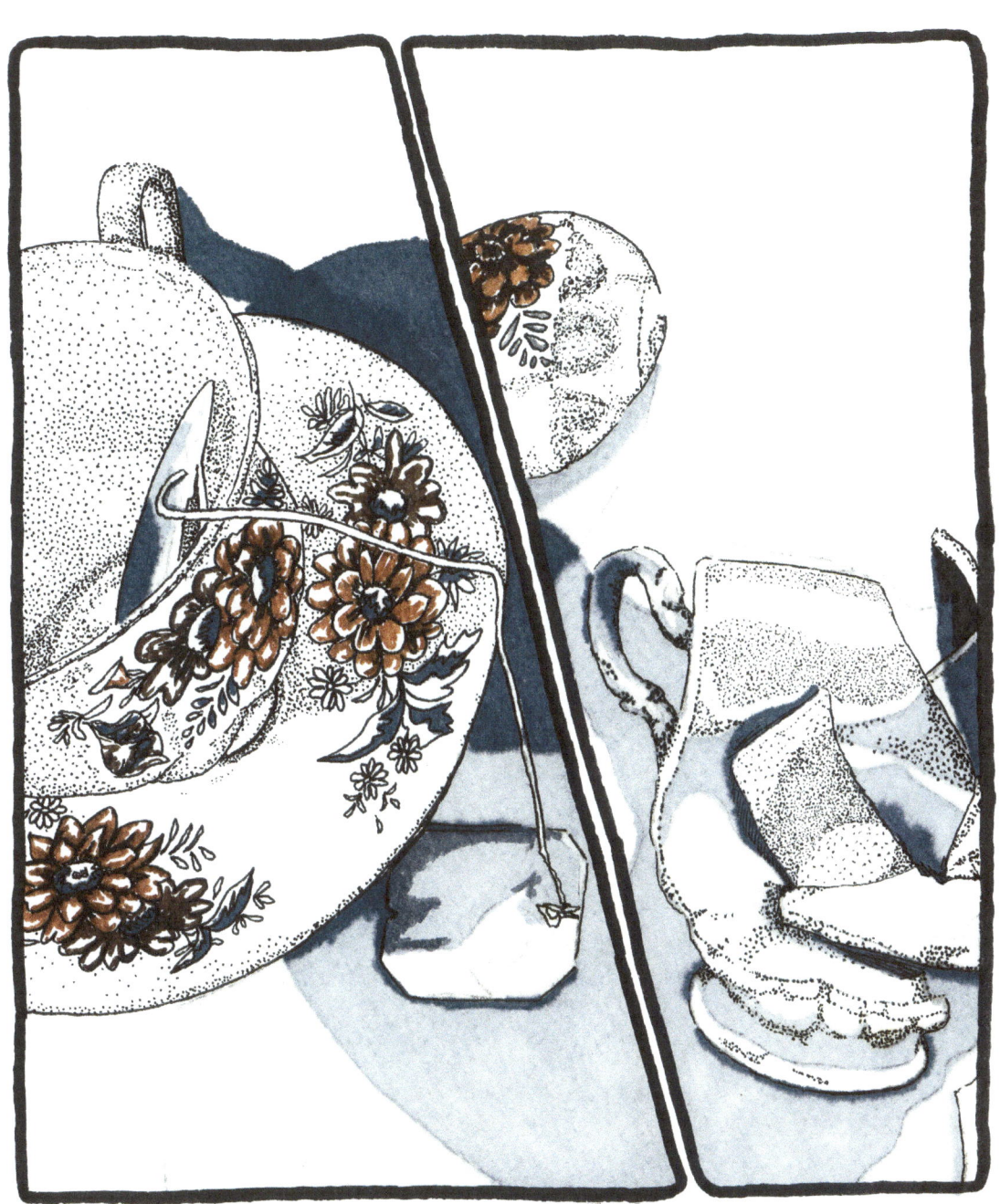

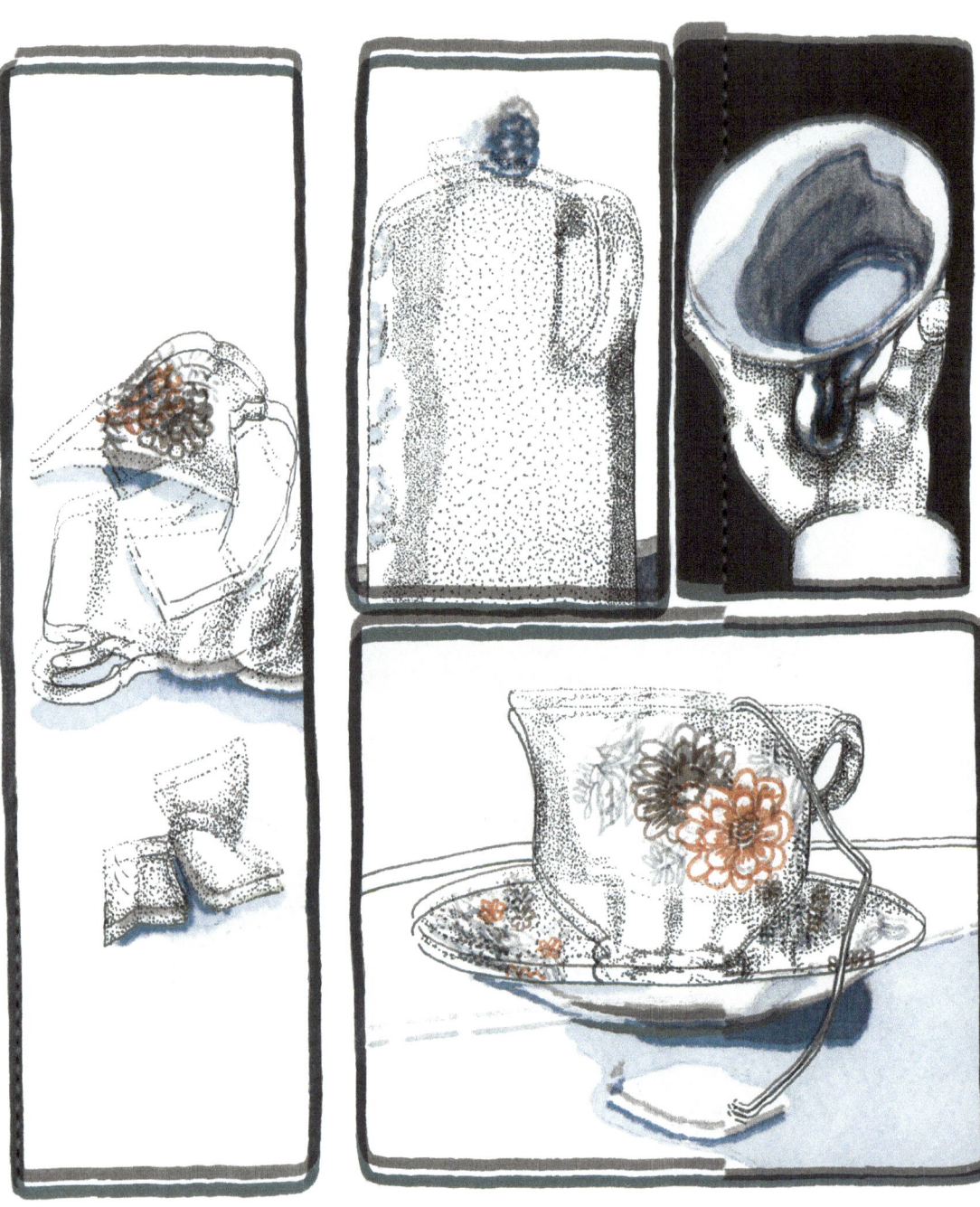

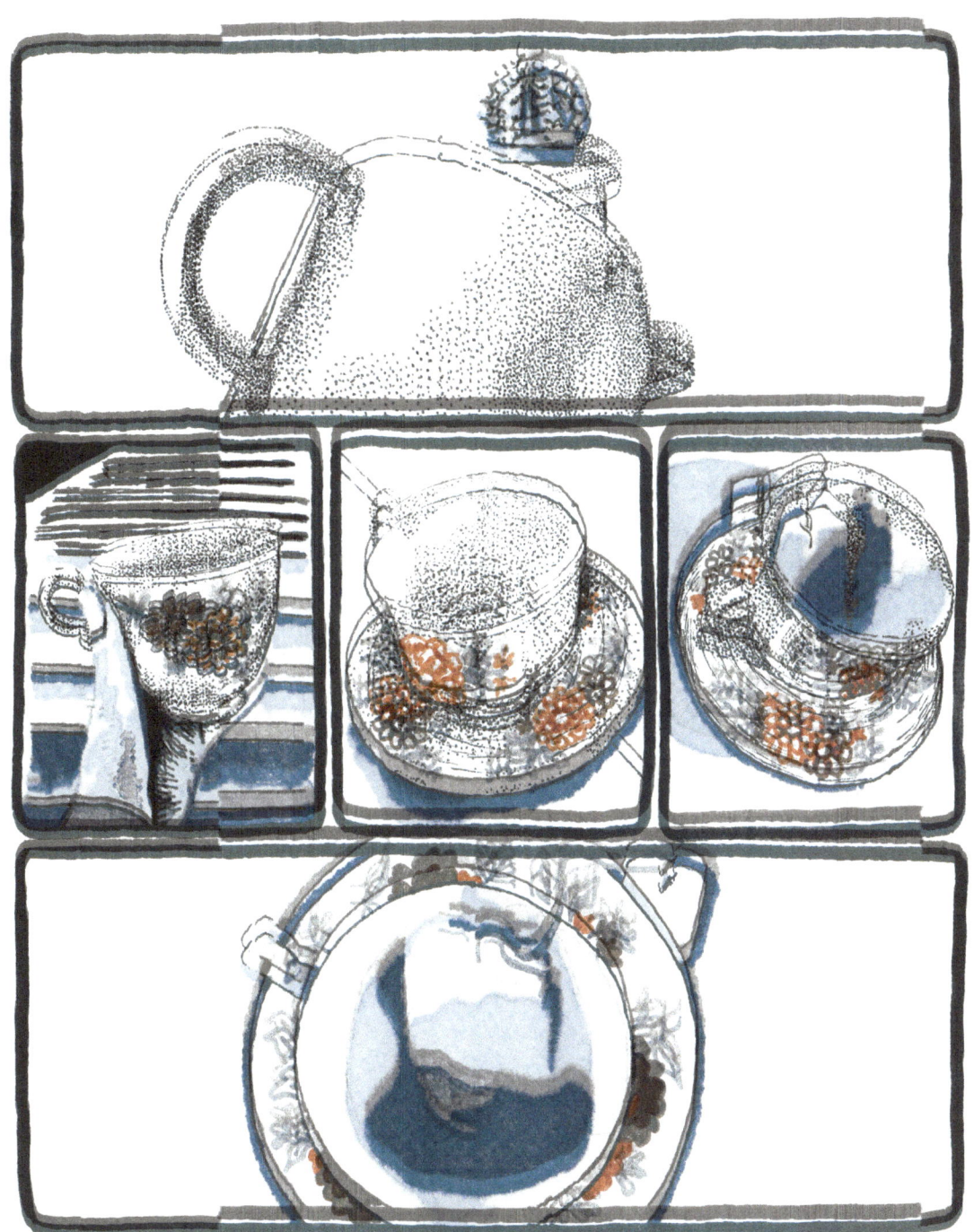

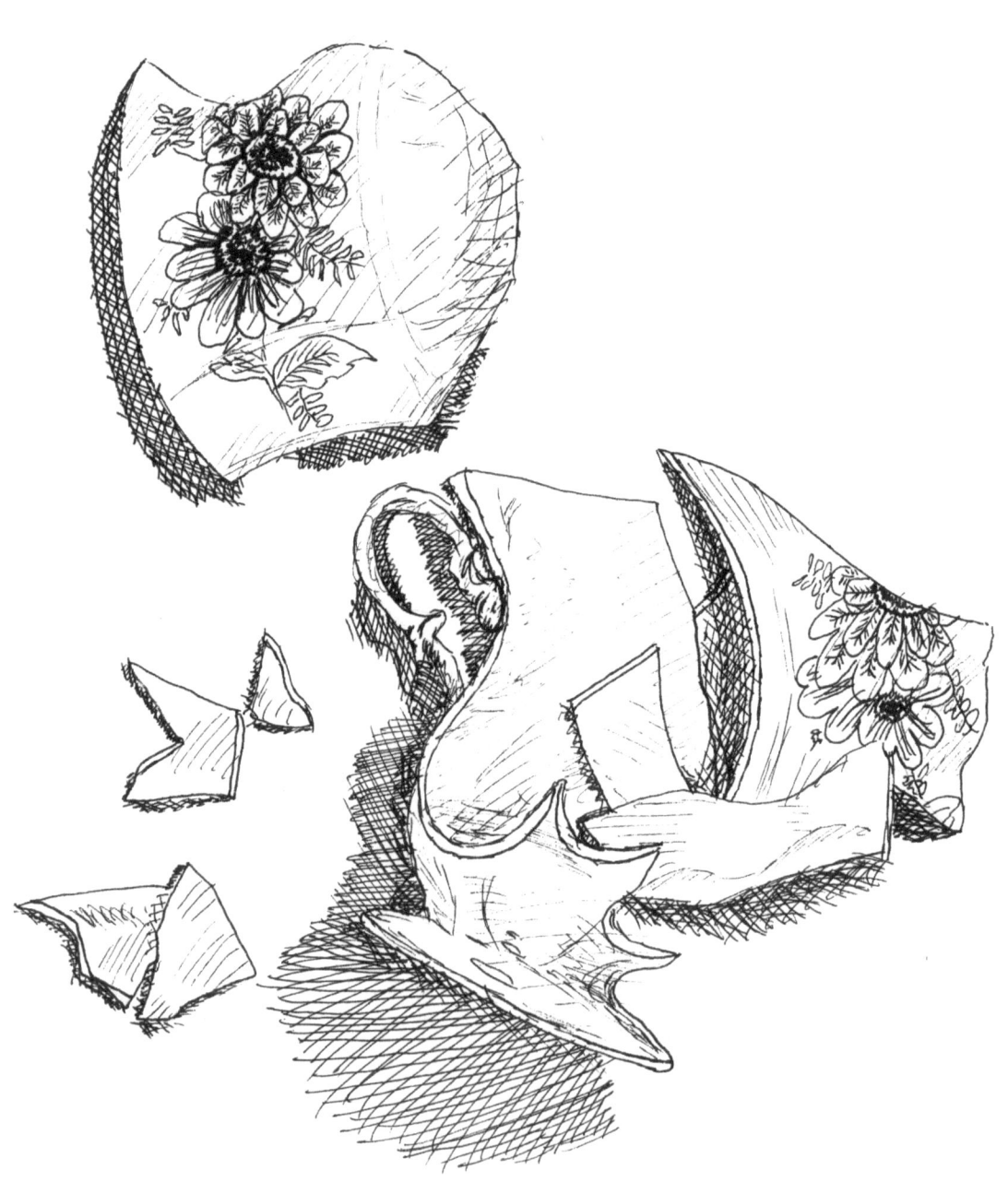

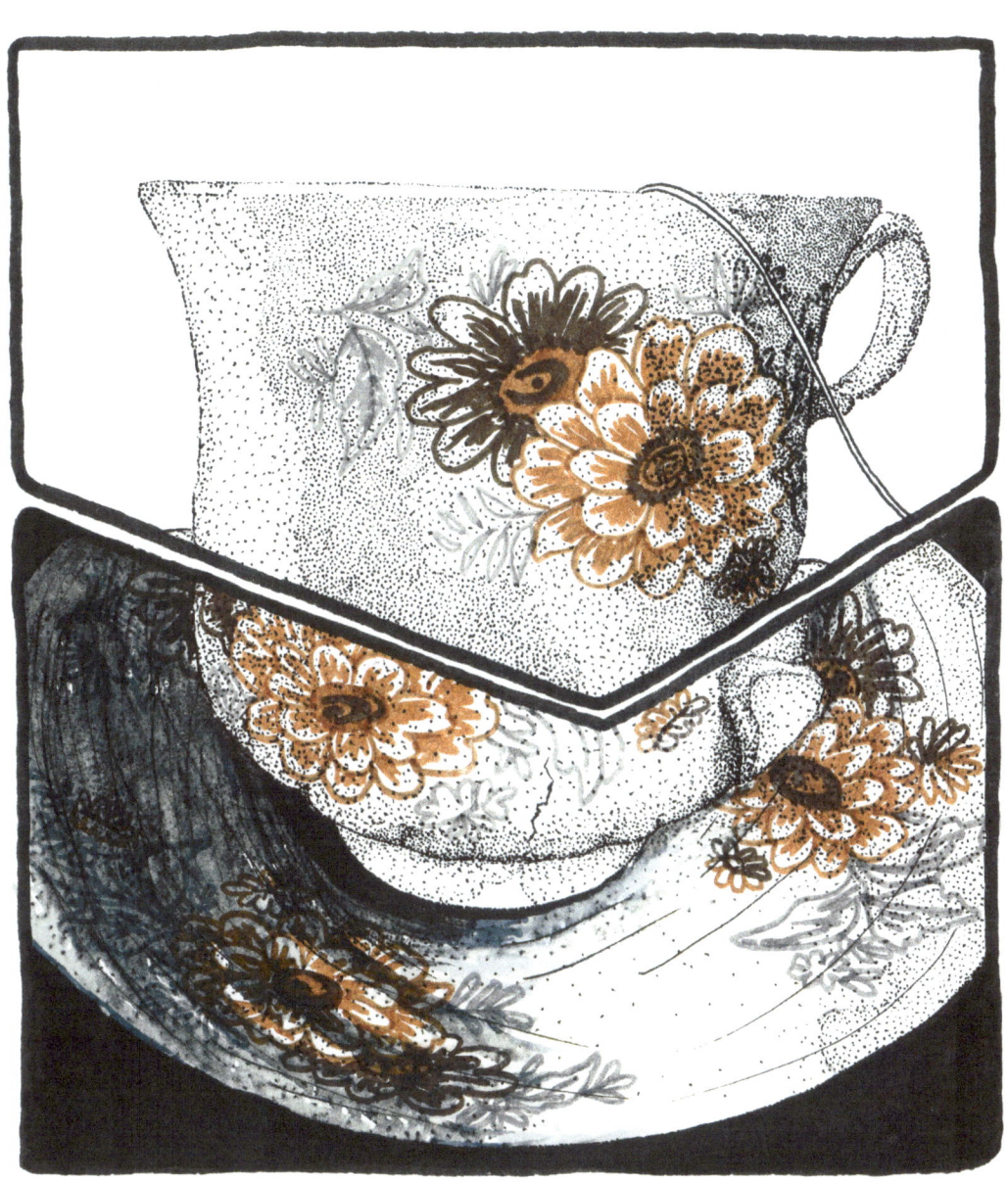

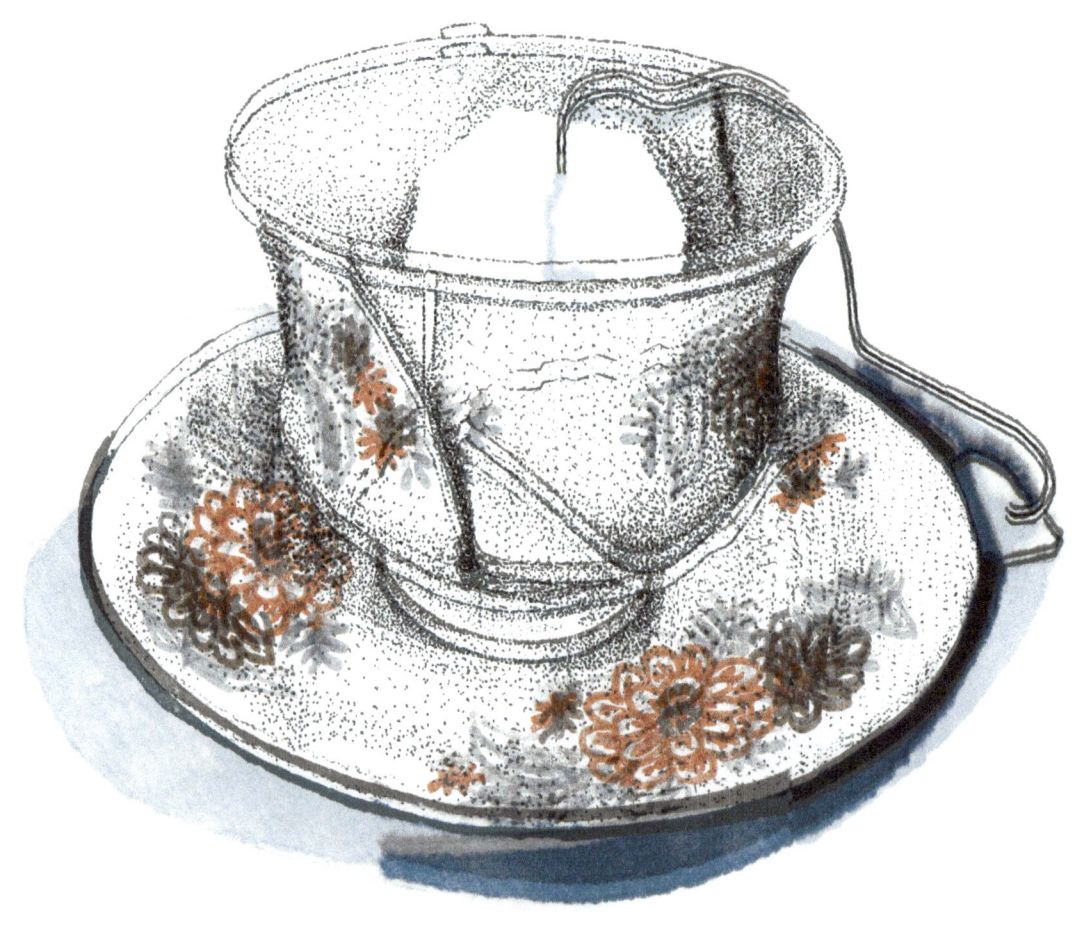

One of the fondest memories I have of my Grandmother is sitting down with her, while she had a cup of tea, and we both ate a piece or two of her fresh baked bread. It was over the cup of tea that held to warm her hands, we would laugh.

My Grandmother has since developed Alzheimer's, so now those memories are mine to hold on to.

Tea for One is about memory, all these little changes that happen, and the connections we try to make. Each drawing works together to tell this story through the act of making a cup of tea. Often the images are disjointed. Different images almost connecting together as you try to remember how the cup broke among all the embedded ritual memories of the hundreds of times you've gotten a cup of tea. There are chips gone and pieces jutting out that just won't go back together quite right.

The cup may no longer hold things the way it once did, and you can't put water in it anymore, but it'll hold your teabag just the same as always.

SUNBEAMS

For those moments when you're a cat in the sun, watching the light travel around the room.

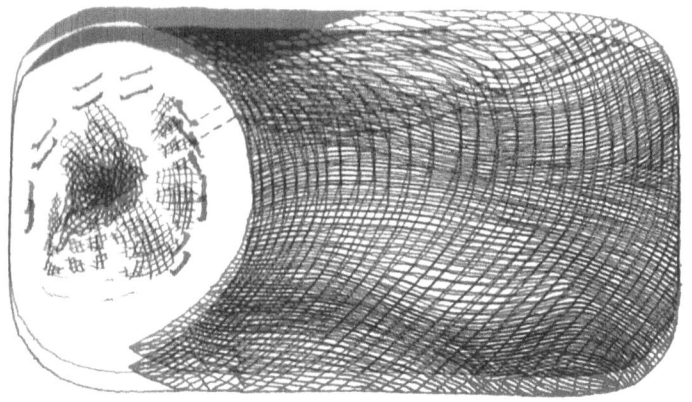
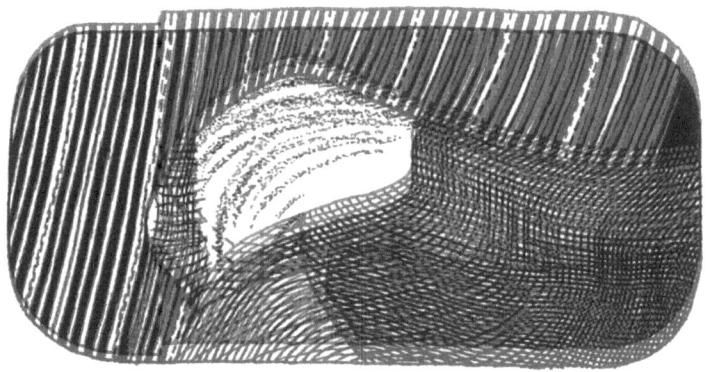
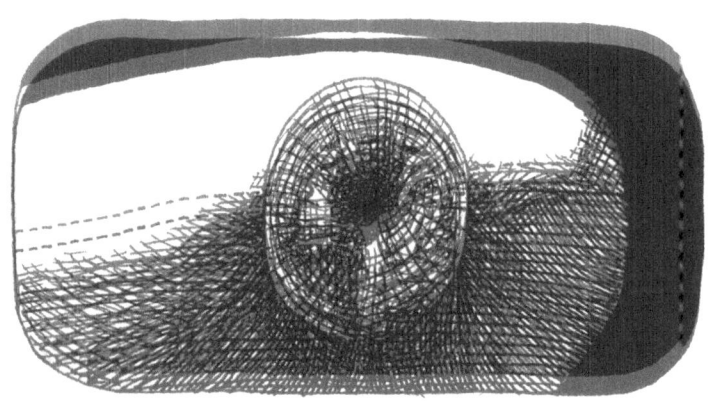

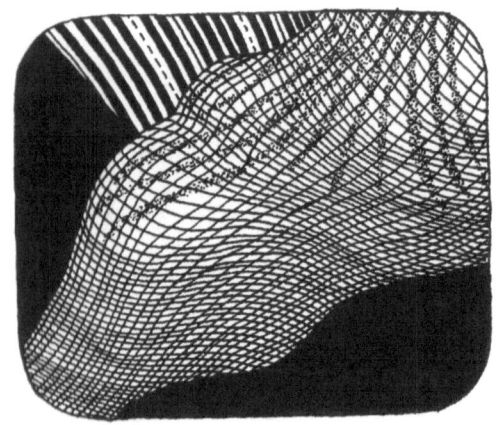
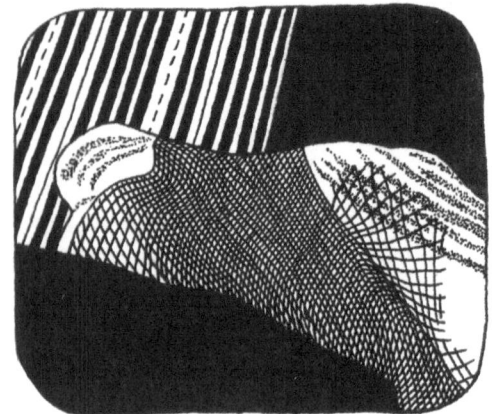
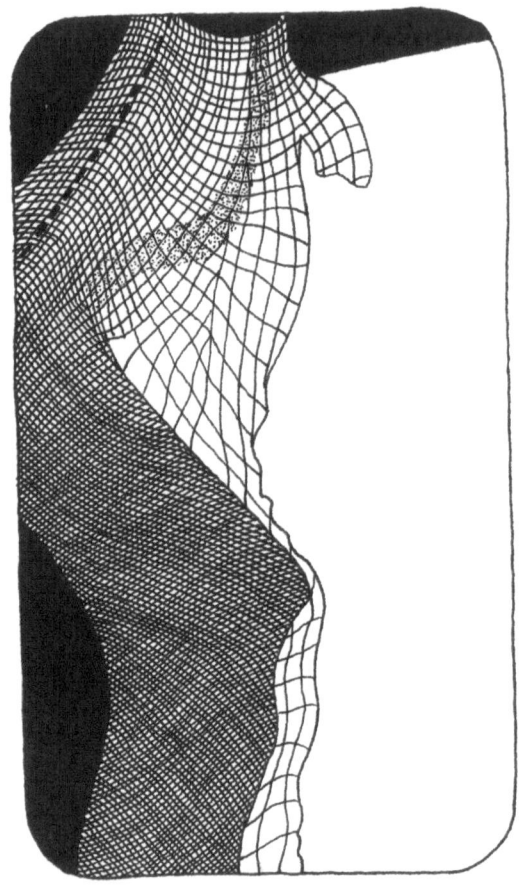
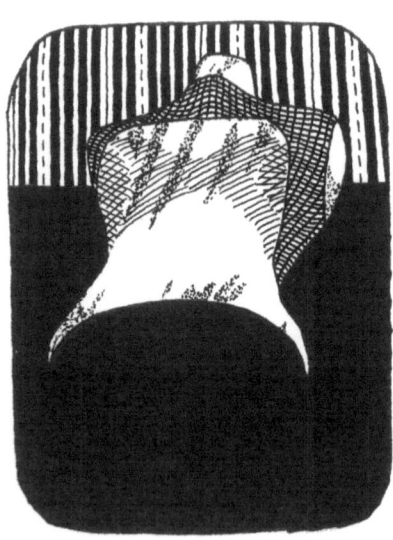
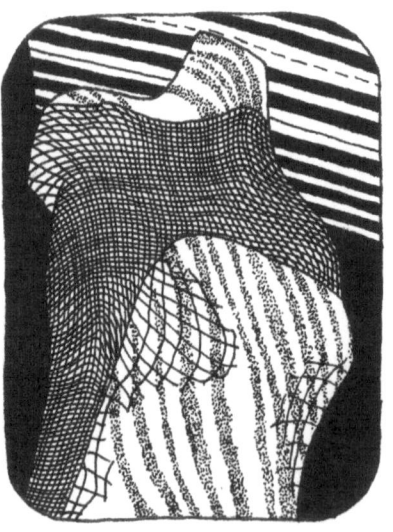

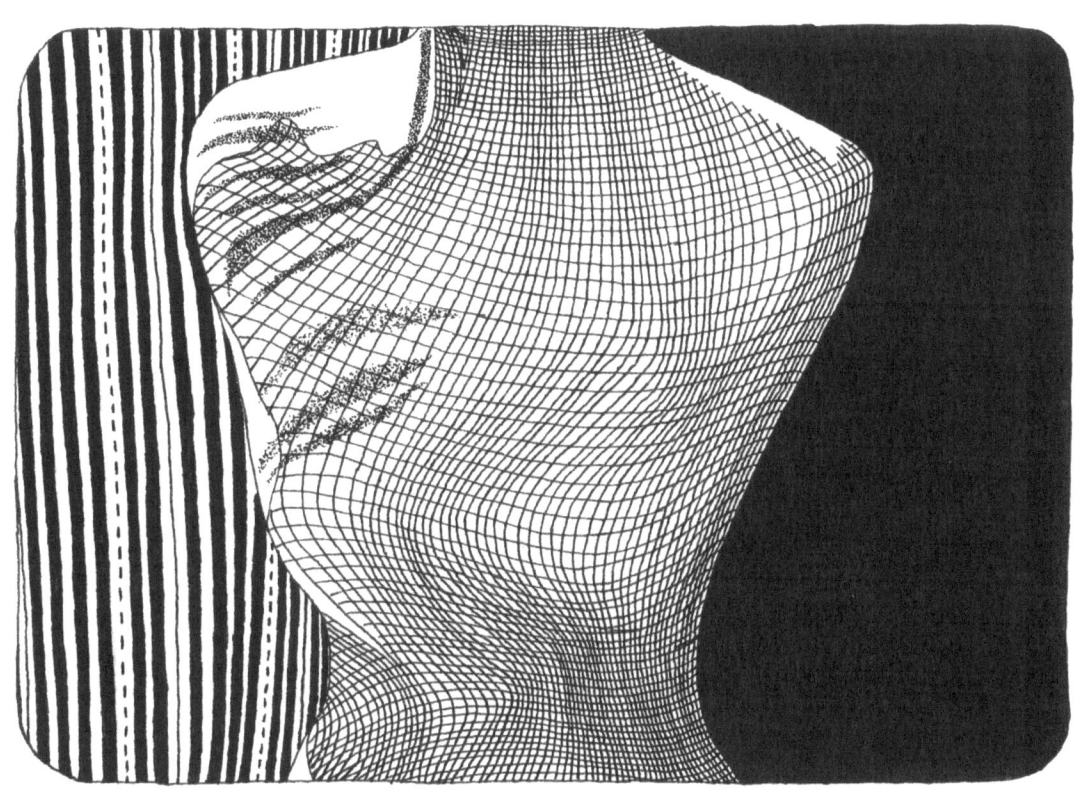

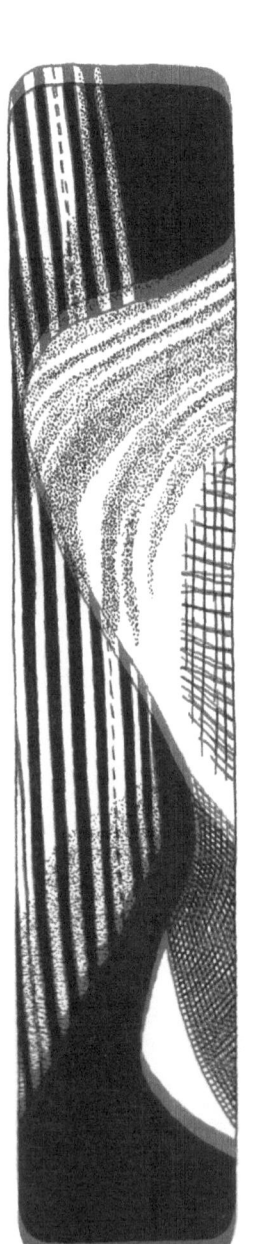
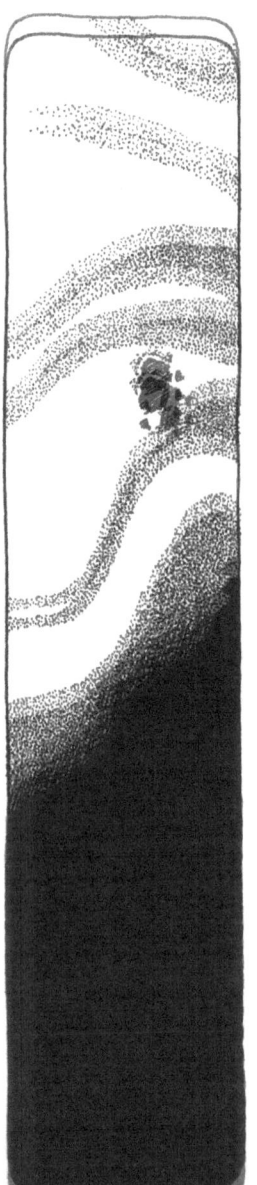
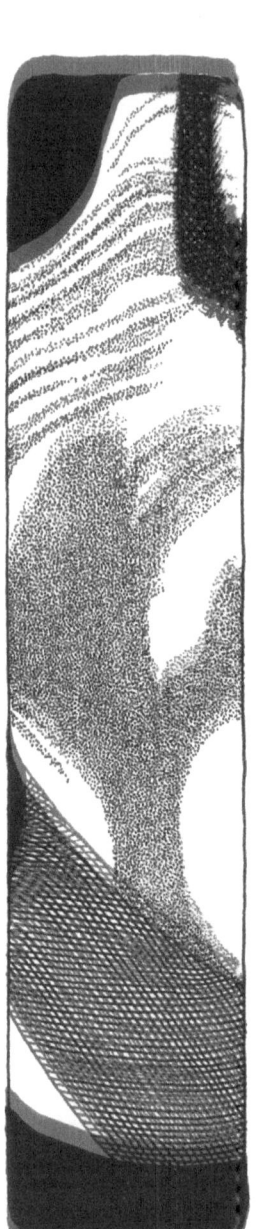
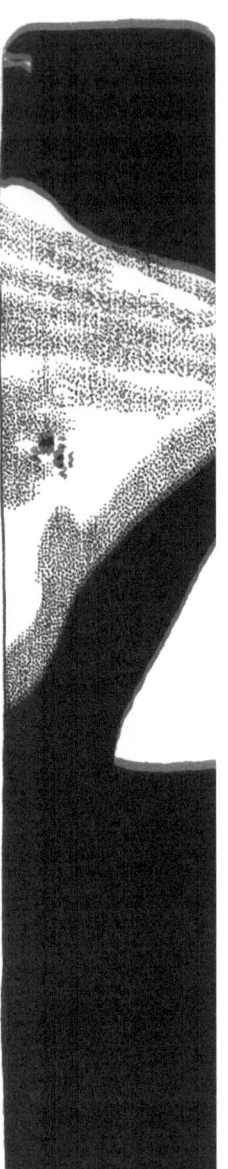

Something

deep

down

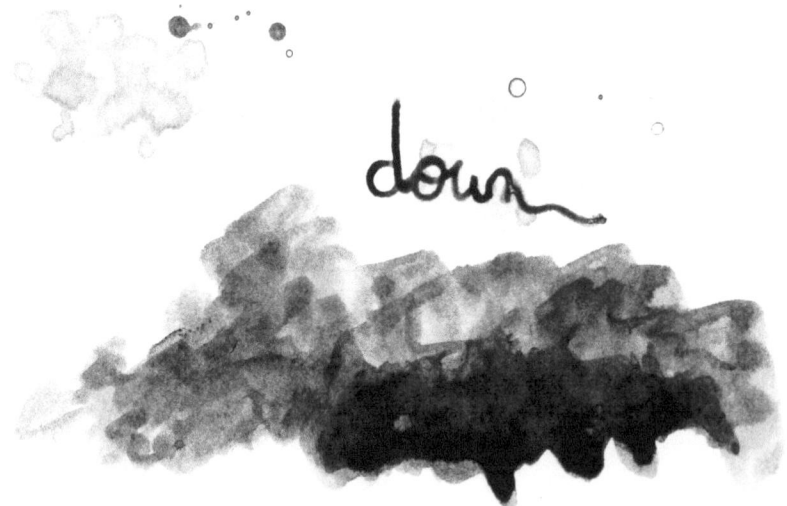

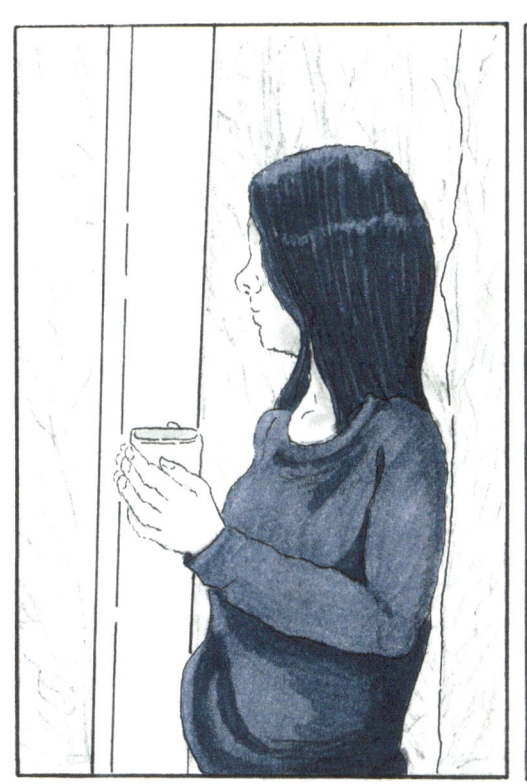
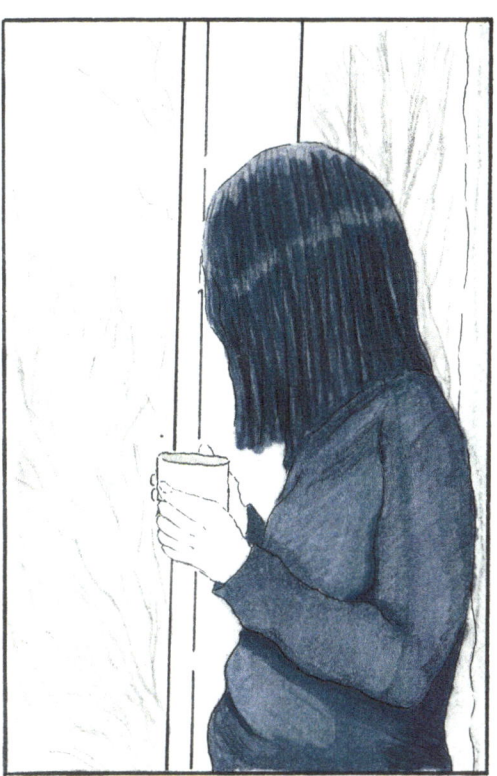
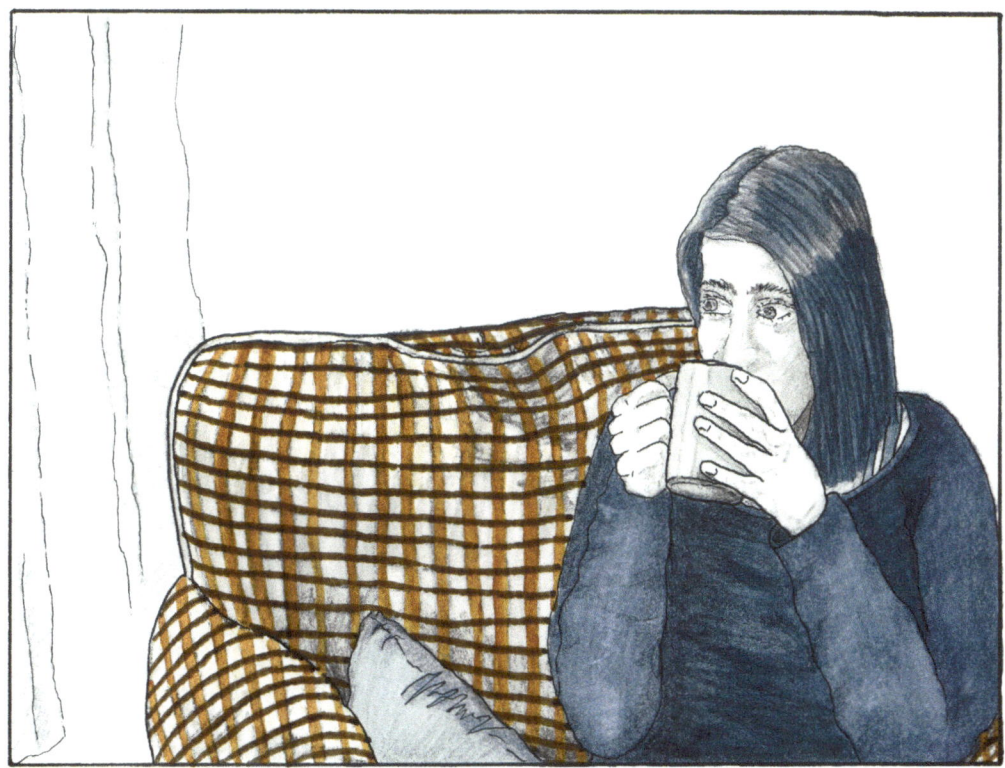

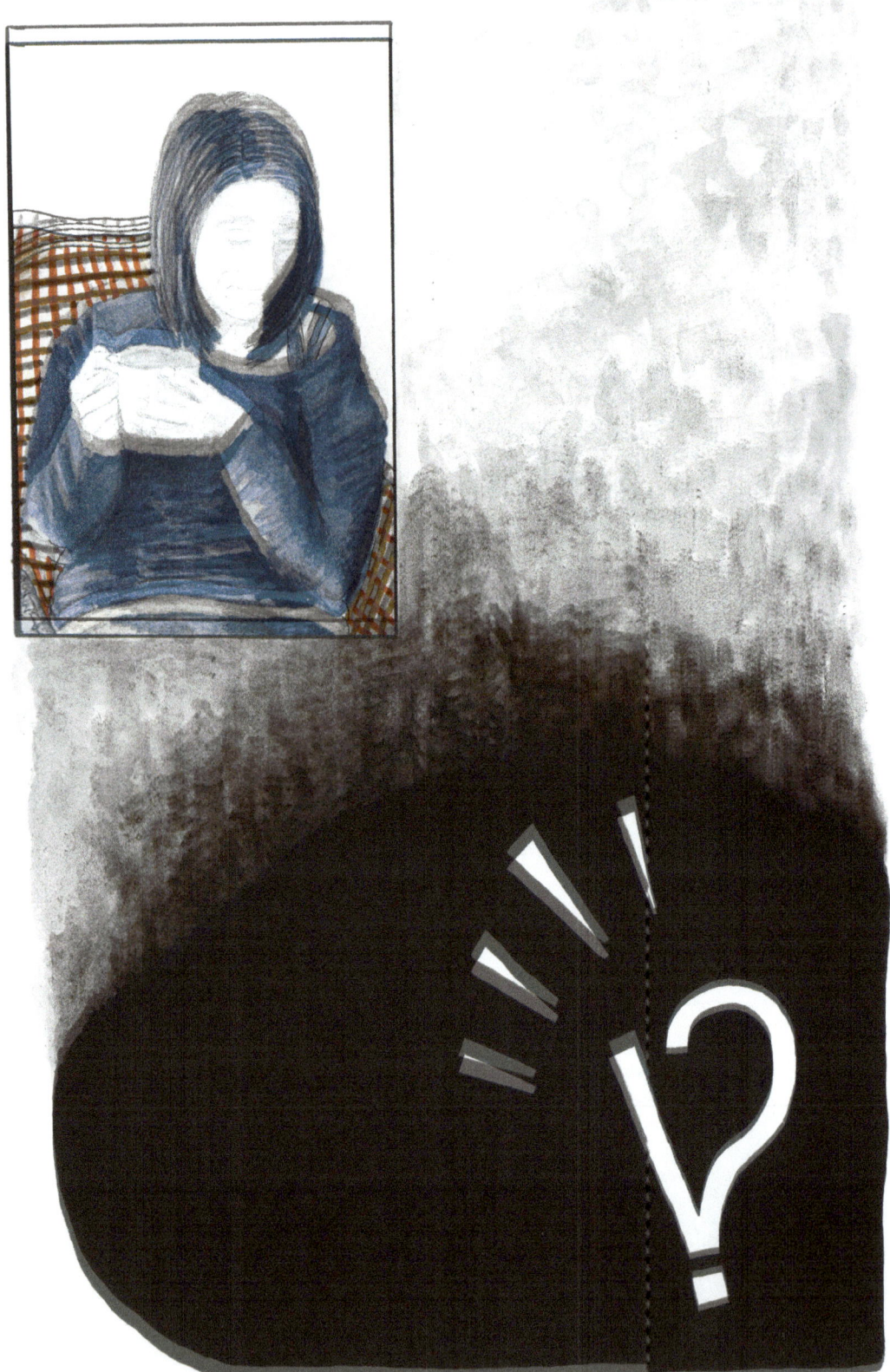

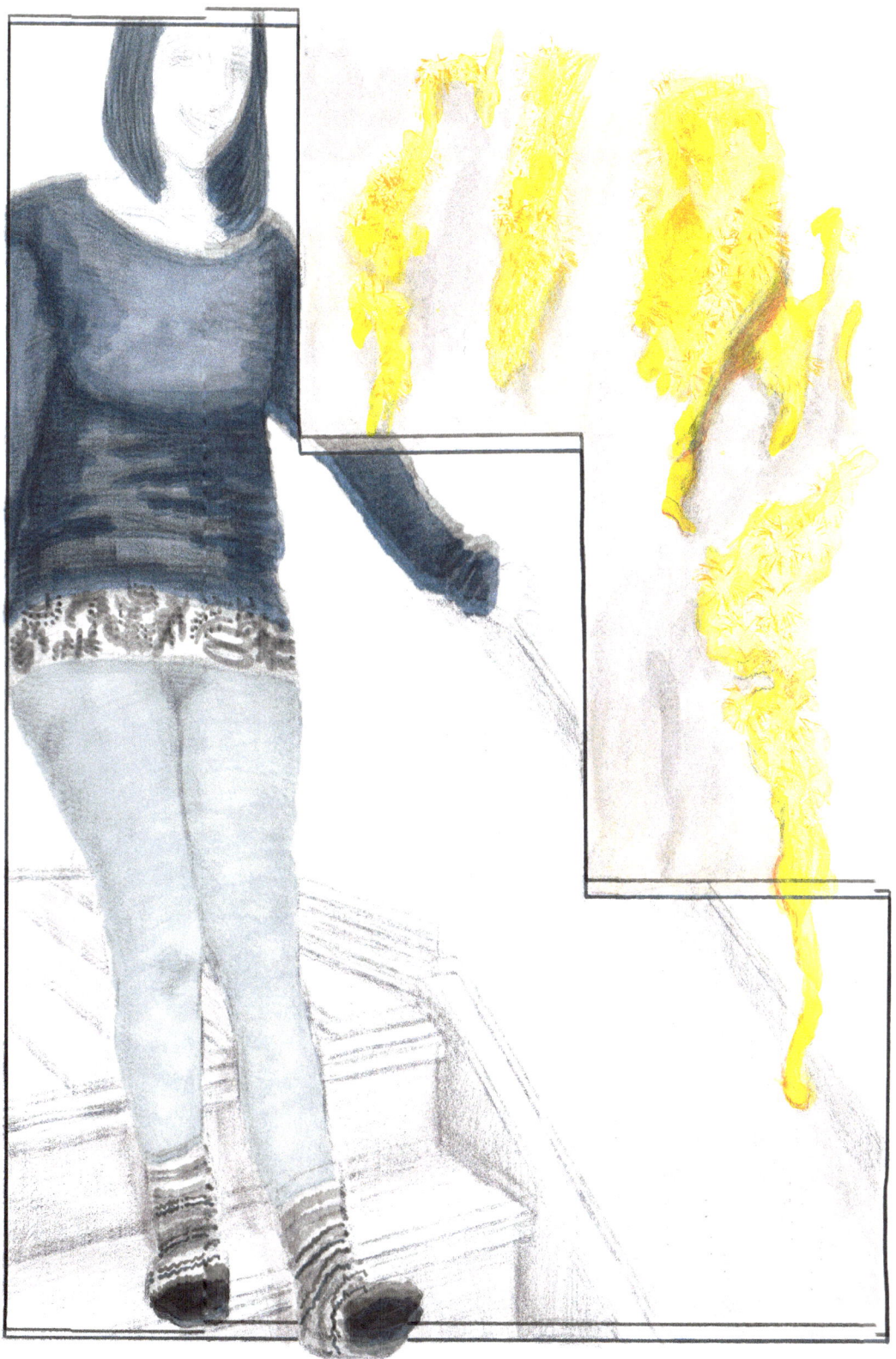

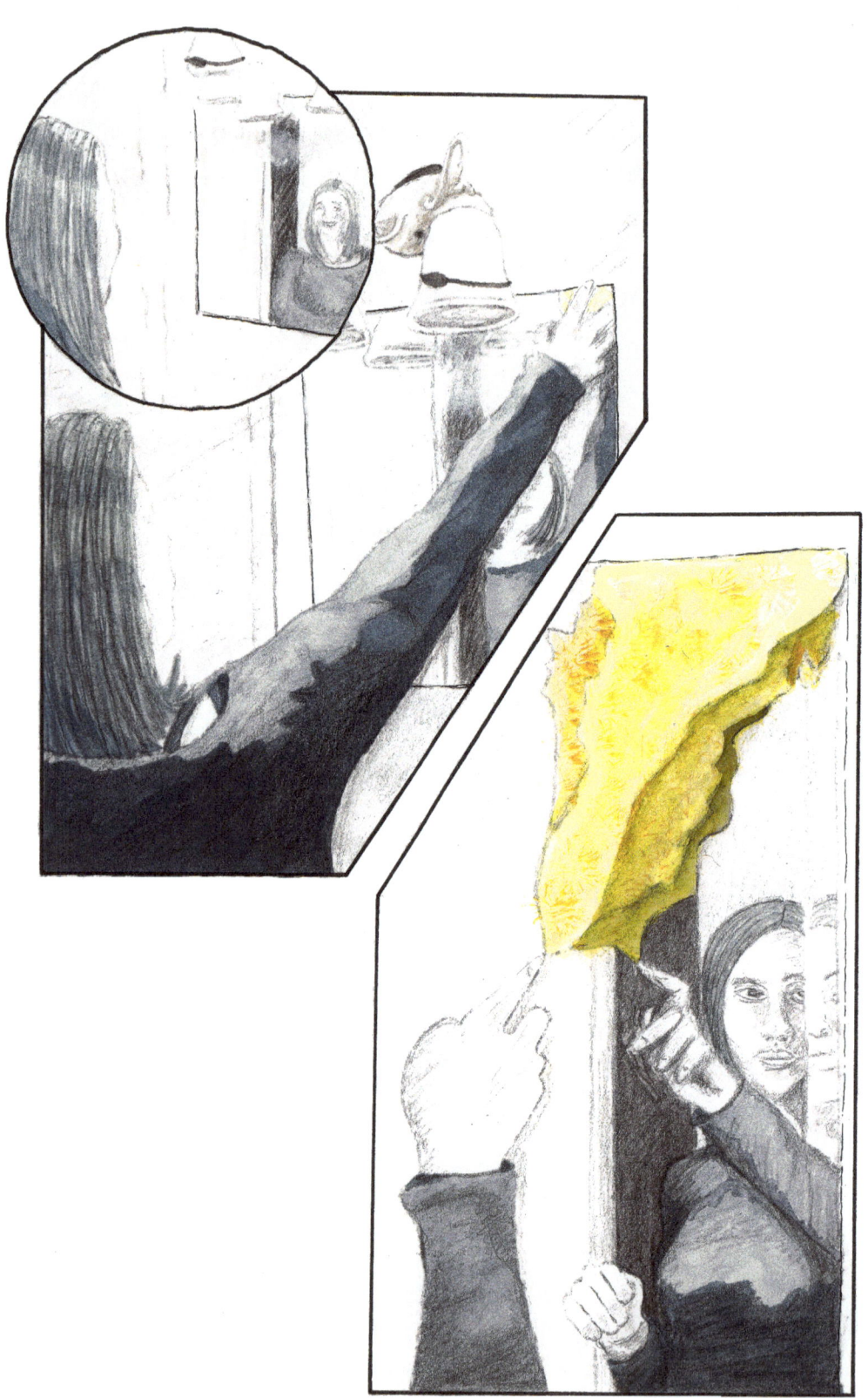

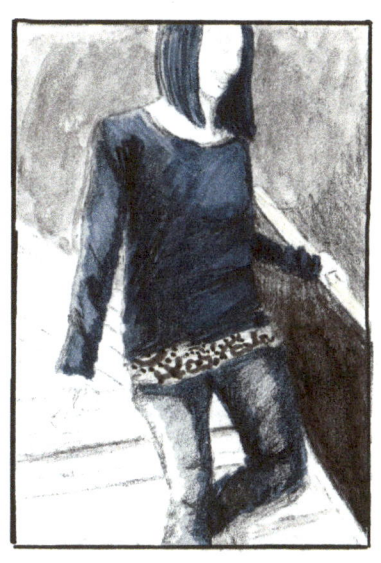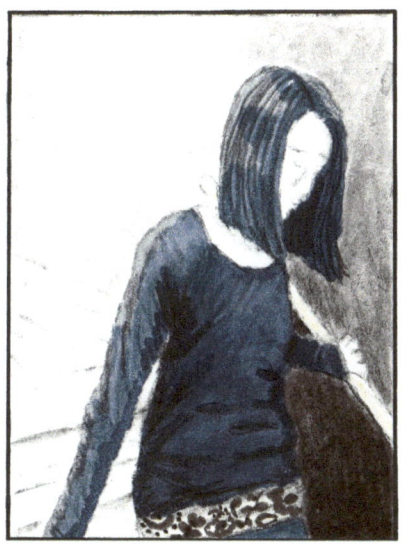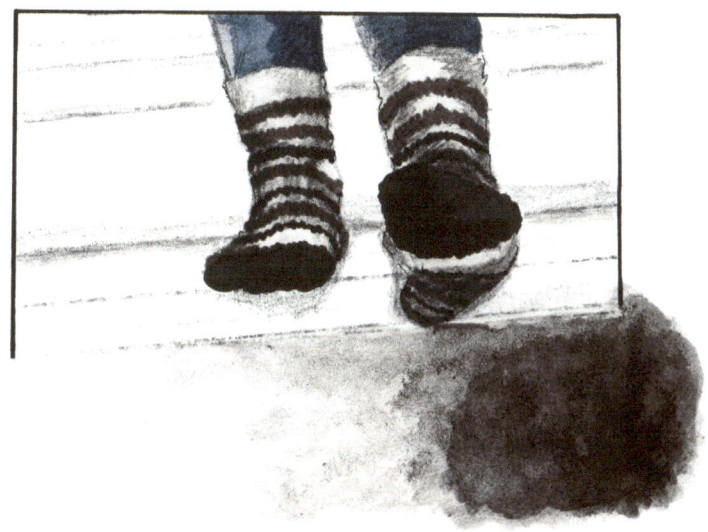

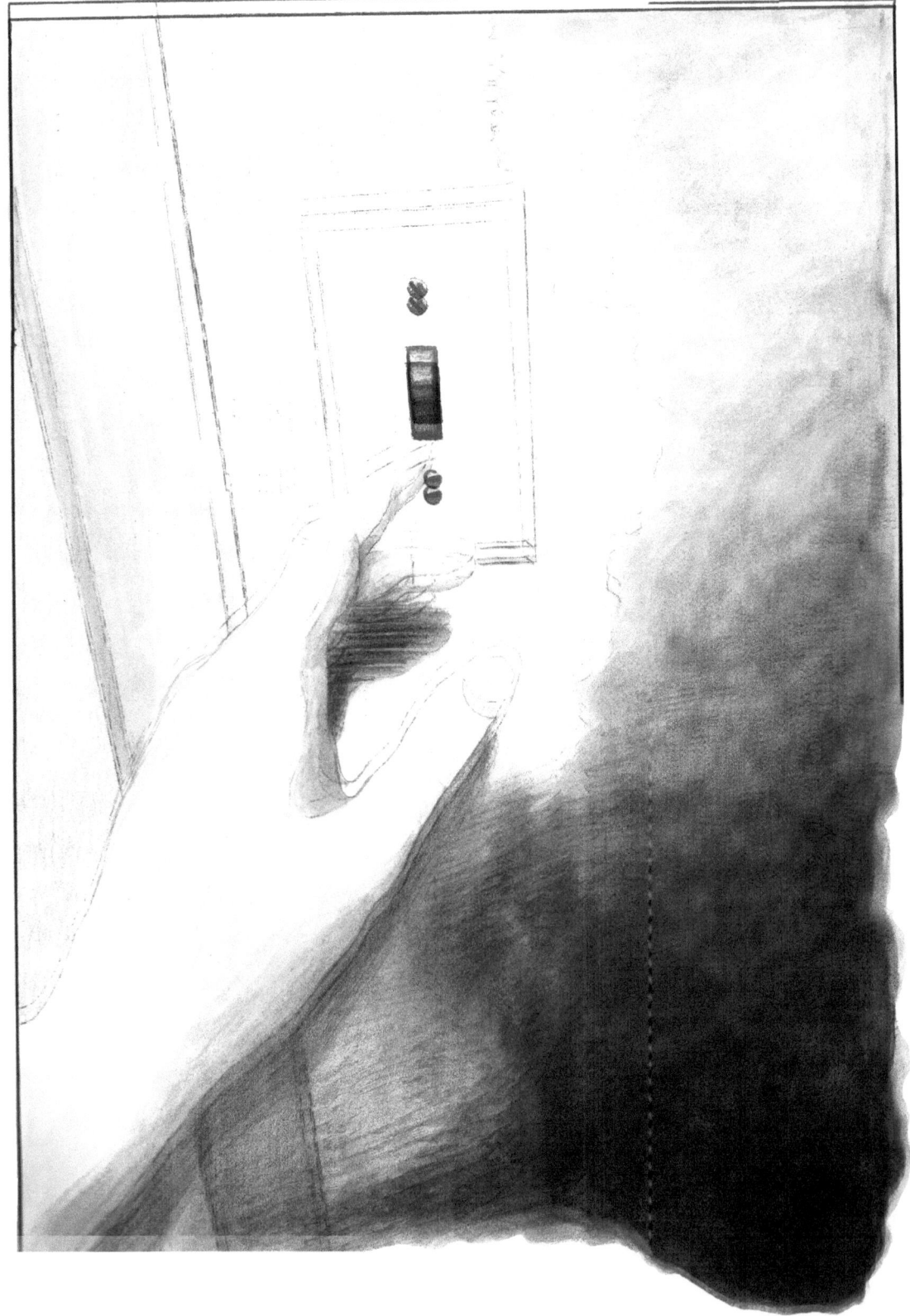

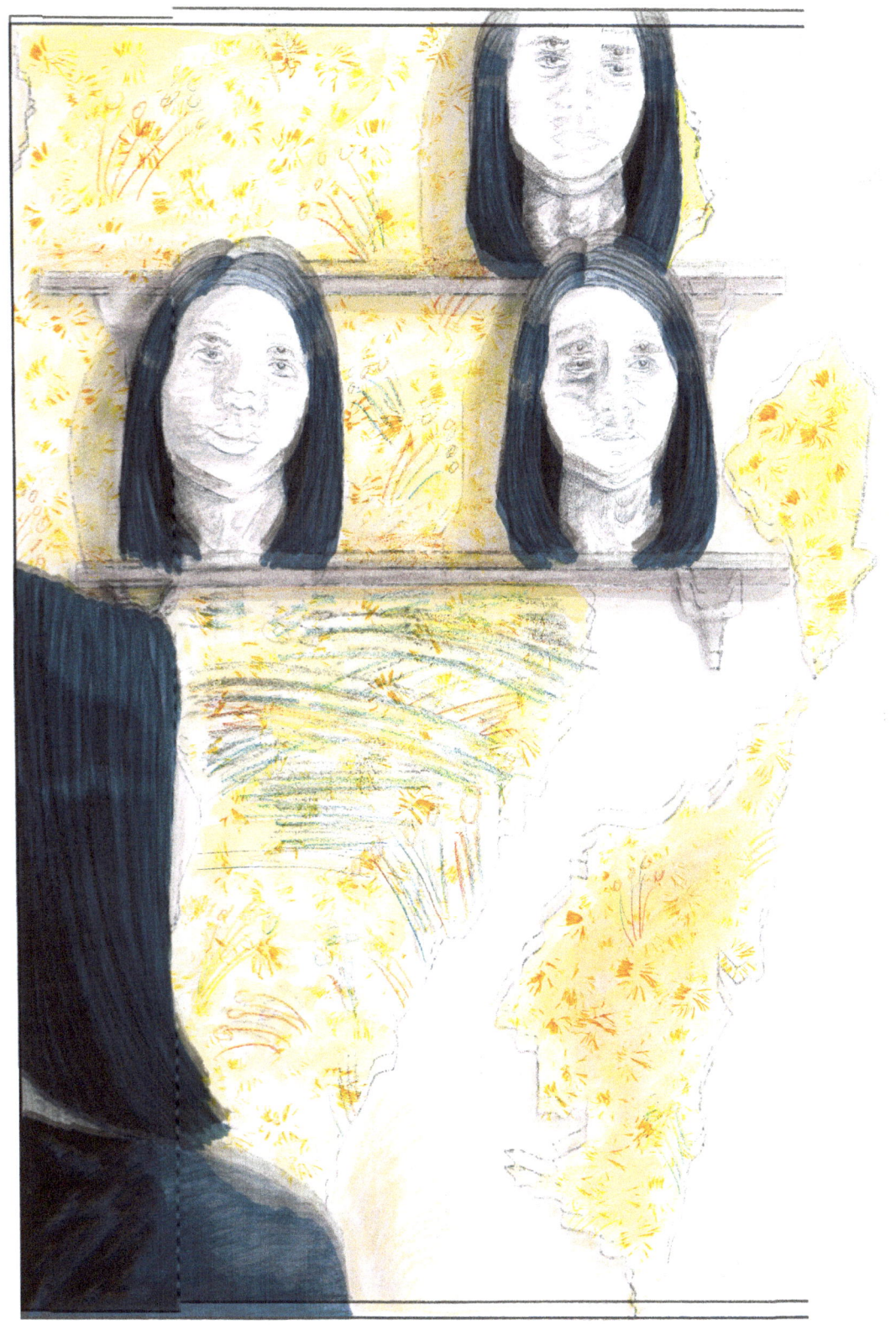

In this piece, we follow a woman through an exploration of herself. Her thoughts and emotions, though kept hidden, can't be kept quiet.

As she travels downwards, walls and fixed solid lines soon give way to vague shapes and shadows - the uncertainty showing with a shifting face.

As lines blur and layers peel, we move ever onward, ultimately illuminating what awaits within.

www.ingramcontent.com/pod-product-compliance
Lightning Source LLC
Chambersburg PA
CBHW051938210526
45473CB00006B/2298